GLOBAL
WARMING

Essential Viewpoints

GLOBAL
WARMING

BY AMY FARRAR

Content Consultant
Dr. Michael D. Mastrandrea, Research Associate
Center for Environmental Science and Policy, Stanford University

ABDO
Publishing Company

CREDITS

Published by ABDO Publishing Company, 8000 West 78th Street, Edina, Minnesota 55439. Copyright © 2008 by Abdo Consulting Group, Inc. International copyrights reserved in all countries. No part of this book may be reproduced in any form without written permission from the publisher. The Essential Library™ is a trademark and logo of ABDO Publishing Company.

Printed in the United States.

Editors: Nadia Higgins, Thomas Parmalee, Patricia Stockland
Cover design: Becky Daum
Interior design: Lindaanne Donohoe

Library of Congress Cataloging-in-Publication Data
Farrar, Amy.
  Global warming / Amy Farrar.
     p. cm. — (Essential viewpoints)
  Includes bibliographical references and index.
  ISBN 978-1-59928-859-8
  1. Global warming—Juvenile literature. I. Title.

QC981.8.G56F378 2008
  363.738'74—dc22

                              2007013879

TABLE OF CONTENTS

Former Vice President Al Gore discusses the dangers of global warming while touring Glacier National Park.

A WARMER WORLD

For more than 100 years, people have been visiting Glacier National Park in northern Montana. Visitors hike and camp, wade in streams and lakes fed by glacier water, and view abundant wildlife. One of the most popular activities is driving a scenic

route to see massive glaciers and the rugged landscape that they shaped thousands of years ago.

Glaciers are large, slow-moving sheets of snow, ice, and rock debris that can fill valleys or cover entire continents, such as Antarctica. Glaciers accumulate over hundreds or thousands of years. In 1850, when glaciers worldwide expanded at the end of "The Little Ice Age," 150 glaciers covered northern Montana's landscape. Today, only 27 glaciers remain at Glacier National Park.

As Earth's temperature slowly began to rise in the late 1880s, glaciers in Montana and other areas around the globe started to retreat. Earth's warming has continued due to a process commonly referred to as global warming. A simple definition of global warming is a continuing increase in Earth's overall temperature. The planet's surface temperature has increased approximately 1.4 degrees Fahrenheit (0.76° C) in the last 150 years. This increase is an average. In some areas, temperatures may have increased by as much as 5 degrees Fahrenheit (2.8° C), and in other areas, temperatures may have stayed the same or even decreased.

Preserving Beauty

Glacier National Park officially joined the U.S. national park system in 1910, as the nation's tenth park. The park supports scientific research, including the Global Climate Change program.

Unprecedented Warming

Caspar Ammann of the National Center for Atmospheric Research said global warming "continues at a rate we have not seen for 10,000 years."[1] To compare today's warming to the past, Ammann pointed to the last glacial period that took place around 20,000 years ago. He said that from that point until now, Earth's average temperature has increased only ten degrees Fahrenheit (6° C)—a rate much slower than reflected in the past 120 years.

Historically, Earth's temperature has gone up and down in a natural cycle, and such an abrupt temperature increase is not unheard of in Earth's history, he concedes. However, the current warming is happening at a point in the natural cycle in which the planet would normally be cooling off. Instead, "we are now warming up even more," he said.[2]

GREENHOUSE GASES

The Earth's atmosphere contains 78 percent nitrogen and 21 percent oxygen. The remaining one percent includes greenhouse gases such as carbon dioxide, methane, nitrous oxide, and ozone. These greenhouse gases trap heat inside the atmosphere. They work like a glass roof that traps heat inside a greenhouse or windows that trap heat inside a car on a hot day.

Greenhouse gases have been essential to the survival of the planet. Without them, the average temperature on Earth would be just 0.4 degrees Fahrenheit (-18° C). That would be too cold to sustain most life.

Since around the 1850s, however, human activity has significantly increased the amount of greenhouse gases—in particular, carbon dioxide. This increase has been the driving cause of global warming. What activities contribute to global warming? Burning fossil fuels such as coal, petroleum

(oil), and natural gas is the main cause. Almost half of the power plants in the United States generate electricity by burning coal. Many homes are heated by natural gas, and gasoline for cars and trucks comes from petroleum. The clear-cutting and burning of forests are other factors. These practices harm the environment by emitting excess carbon dioxide into the atmosphere.

HEART OF THE ISSUE

The heart of the debate about global warming has recently shifted. People used to dispute whether global warming was even occurring, but the data clearly show that Earth is becoming warmer. Another topic of debate had to do with the causes of global warming. Historically, Earth's temperature has gone up and down in a natural cycle, so many considered the current warming to be part of a natural process. While a small minority of people still question whether humans are truly responsible for global warming, scientists now

Fossil Fuels

Millions of years ago, even before the dinosaurs, tiny sea animals and plants died on the ocean floor. As time passed, layers of silt, sand, and mud covered the plants and animals deeper and deeper. Over the course of millions of years, heat and pressure from the earth turned them into fossil fuels—petroleum, coal, and natural gas.

Fossil fuels, then, are organic matter, or matter that was once alive. Like all organic matter, the fuels are carbon-based. That is why fossil fuels give off carbon dioxide when they burn.

Middle-School Students Worry About the Warming

Most people agree that global warming exists. But there is still widespread disagreement on how dangerous it is. It may be surprising to learn that a recent survey of 1,000 middle-school students throughout the United States found that almost 60 percent of the students said they feared global warming and environmental disasters more than terrorism, car crashes, and cancer. According to the survey, almost 33 percent of those polled said they thought about global warming a lot.

Stories about children and young adults fearing the worst when it comes to global warming are common. Sean Hussey and his twin sister, Erin, are nine years old, but they worry about polar bears being left homeless. "There are lots of animals that shouldn't die," Erin Hussey said. "The humans are the ones who are causing it."[3]

While global warming may be a serious issue, experts recommend that young adults keep in mind that global warming is a slow process. Lawrence Balter, Professor of Applied Psychology at New York University notes, "There's an opportunity for us to learn about how it works and an opportunity to see if we can do something about it."[4]

Also, people can reduce global warming by limiting energy use, buying an energy-efficient car, and becoming involved in politics to address issues related to global warming.

have overwhelming evidence that this is the case. Today, the debate centers around these questions: How harmful is global warming? What should be done about it?

How Harmful Is It?

To many people, global warming is an immediate danger to the planet. Global warming has been linked to an increase in heat waves and heat-related deaths. It is linked to the melting of Earth's

3 1833 05336 6727

polar ice caps, rising sea levels, and expanding deserts. Increased temperatures also are changing habitats and disrupting ecosystems, which contributes to the extinction or endangering of animals. As temperatures rise, these harmful effects will only worsen. Many believe society will not be able to cope with the negative effects of global warming unless immediate action is taken.

Others, however, believe that society will be able to adapt to the effects of global warming. They believe that temperatures will not increase as much as some fear. They argue that Earth has coped with climate changes in the past, and it will do so again. To this argument, others counter that the current rate of global warming is unprecedented. It is extremely unlikely that climate changes in the past 10,000 years have been as rapid as the changes in the past 150 years. It is harder for the planet to adapt to changes that happen so quickly.

What Should Be Done?

Many point to alternative energies, such as wind and solar energy, as a way to replace fossil fuels and reduce greenhouse gases. They also urge people to save energy by turning off lights or carpooling. Others argue that alternative energy is just too expensive to produce or too unreliable to depend on in the near future. Society should focus on ways to use fossil fuels that do not release greenhouse gases into the atmosphere, by trapping the gases underground or deep in the ocean. Still others believe that the costs of taking drastic action are just too high. They believe that society will be in a better position to make drastic changes later on, when, for example, alternative energy technology is more advanced.

An Inconvenient Truth?

Former vice president Al Gore shares the belief that global warming is an immediate concern. He helped bring the potential dangers of global warming to the public's attention with his book, *An Inconvenient Truth*. In 2006, the book was turned into a documentary film by the same name. The book reached number three on the *New York Times* bestseller list, and the movie played to packed theaters, which is rare for a documentary. The book and film paint a grim picture of

Global Warming Can Boost Insurance Costs

Global warming may not only harm the environment, it can also boost insurance costs. According to a 2005 study, global warming could lead to an increase in severe storms, flooding, infectious diseases, and other problems that could make health insurance and insurance against natural disasters more expensive.

"We found that impacts of climate change are likely to lead to ramifications that overlap in several areas including our health, our economy and the natural systems on which we depend," said Paul Epstein, the study's lead author and associate director of the Center for Health and the Global Environment at Harvard Medical School.[5]

Earth's future. If nothing is done to slow or reduce global warming, Gore says that the world will see more deadly storms such as Hurricane Katrina, more droughts, and more retreating glaciers. The streets of New York City could be flooded. At the same time, Gore insists that even simple actions such as using energy-efficient light bulbs can slow global warming.

Most climate scientists lauded Gore for his work. "He got all the important material and got it right," said William Schlesinger of Duke University's School of Environmental and Earth Sciences.[6]

But not everyone was this enthusiastic. Some took issue with his coverage of Hurricane Katrina. "I thought the use of imagery from Hurricane Katrina was inappropriate and unnecessary," said Brian Soden, a professor of meteorology and oceanography at the University of Miami. "There are plenty of disturbing impacts associated with global warming for which there is much greater scientific consensus," he said.[7]

Some, including President George W. Bush, thought that the disaster scenarios presented in the film were little more than scare tactics. In fact, the president refused to even view the film. Others, such as Tom Wigley of the National Center for Atmospheric Research, accused Gore of presenting too simple of an approach. In Wigley's opinion, global warming will not be slowed through simple conservation efforts.

As scientists study the path to global warming, they find more factors pointing to human causes. The debate over how to reverse these effects becomes more heated. And some people question whether it is even possible to slow or reverse the climate changes being studied.

In January 2004, former vice president Al Gore delivered an address on global warming in which he called for better environmental policies.

The natural habitat of penguins has been reduced by global warming.

THE PATH TO GLOBAL WARMING

ince its beginnings 4.6 billion years ago, Earth's climate has varied widely. During ice ages, much of North America was covered in glaciers. In between ice ages, global temperatures have been as high as they are now. These changes in Earth's

climate were due to a number of natural causes. Changes in the sun's intensity and in Earth's position relative to the sun affected temperatures. Massive volcanic eruptions and increases in plant and animal life have also increased carbon dioxide levels in the atmosphere.

For these reasons, it took scientists several decades to figure out that the most recent global warming has been caused not by natural forces but by human activities. As scientists examined and debated the evidence, it became clear that this climate change was significantly different from those in the past. Never in human history has Earth warmed up so quickly before and for such an extended period of time. Greenhouse gas levels are rising at unprecedented rates as well. In the past, increases in greenhouse gases dropped off after a few years as the excess gases were naturally absorbed. Today, however, carbon dioxide levels have increased by more than a third since the 1850s. Such a rate of increase would have taken thousands of years—not just decades— to occur on its own.

Scientists trace the beginnings of current global warming to the Industrial Revolution, which took place in Europe and North America between 1760 and 1850. The Industrial Revolution signaled a new way of living that increased reliance on machines and factories—and the use of fossil fuels. Scientists started to detect global warming in the late 1800s. By the 1950s, global warming was a significant research topic among climate scientists. The political debate began in earnest in the 1980s.

THE PRICE OF PROGRESS

Before the Industrial Revolution, life was full of hardships. To travel, people either walked or rode horses. Most sewed their own clothes. To heat their homes, people would spend several hours a week chopping wood for their stoves.

The Industrial Revolution made life easier in many respects. People no longer had to farm the land themselves or make their own clothing. Food and fabrics were mass-produced in factories. Inventions such as the steam engine made it possible to travel longer distances on trains. Coal replaced wood as a fuel for heating homes.

Though mechanical wonders made life easier, the Industrial Revolution had a dark side. The coal used to power steam engines in trains, steam ships, and factories released carbon dioxide into the atmosphere. Global warming had begun.

EARLY RESEARCH

In 1824, French philosopher Joseph Fourier described Earth as a giant greenhouse with an atmosphere that traps heat from the sun, making life on Earth possible. But as temperatures began to rise in the late 1800s, Fourier's analogy was largely ignored. People did not understand why it mattered if the planet's temperature increased a degree or two. Swedish chemist Svante Arrhenius studied Fourier's work and discovered in 1896 that levels of carbon dioxide in the atmosphere were related to climate.

Svante Arrhenius

One of the first people to study climate was Svante Arrhenius, a Swedish chemist who began detailed calculations in 1894. During that time, a popular riddle asked how the world cooled during the ice ages. Arrhenius sought to answer that question and hypothesized that gases in the lower atmosphere trapped heat and altered temperatures.

Arrhenius's hard work began. When he finished, he announced that a reduction in atmospheric carbon dioxide levels of between one-third and one-half would result in a global cooling of approximately 8 degrees Fahrenheit (4° C). If the world cooled that much, mass amounts of ice would cover most of the world. Arrhenius had answered the riddle.

But what would happen if the opposite occurred—if the levels of carbon dioxide went up significantly? He did further calculations and concluded that if carbon dioxide levels doubled, worldwide temperatures would increase approximately 10 degrees Fahrenheit (6° C). Decades later, the Intergovernmental Panel on Climate Change, using the most advanced methods known, came up with predictions not too far from Arrhenius's. Modern scientists are amazed at how closely Arrhenius's predictions mirror the climate models of today.

CARBON DIOXIDE EMISSIONS ON THE RISE

It would be many years, however, before the world would take notice of Arrhenius's important findings. Further industrialization and technological developments during the twentieth century only added to greenhouse emissions.

One major contributing factor was the rise of the automobile. In 1908, Henry Ford designed the Model T and mass-produced millions of automobiles in factories. The car became the primary form of transportation, surpassing the train. Because cars run on gasoline, which comes from petroleum, they emit carbon dioxide. As the use of cars spread around the world, greenhouse gases were emitted at unprecedented rates.

Also, the clearing of large tracts of forests to build homes, factories, and businesses further added to the increasing levels of carbon dioxide in the United States. During photosynthesis, trees absorb carbon dioxide through their leaves. When trees are cut or burned, they release this carbon dioxide into the air. Today, the clear-cutting of rain forests in South America and other parts of the world contributes to rising carbon dioxide levels in the air.

MORE RESEARCH

In the 1930s, British steam engineer Guy Callendar took global warming research a step further. He worked out a theory linking greenhouse gas emissions and industrial activity. Callendar collected temperature records from 200 weather stations around the world. The data supported his claim that Earth's overall temperature was indeed increasing. However, Callendar was not dismayed by the results. Instead, he believed that the warming caused by the burning of fossil fuels would be good for humanity, as it lengthened growing seasons.

Beginning in 1958, Charles Keeling and Roger Revelle conducted another landmark study. The two collected air samples from many places in the world every day for years. Revelle and Keeling tried to collect samples from diverse regions of the world. They measured the concentration of carbon dioxide in the samples. Keeling then created a

Increasing Wildfires

Some people blame global warming for making wildfires more frequent and more intense across the United States. There are two main reasons climate change is thought to have such an effect. First, warmer temperatures increase the rate of evaporation of water from plants and trees. So they dry out, making them more vulnerable to fire. Secondly, cold weather helps control the bark beetle population. Because of early snowmelt, four or five generations of the beetles are now able to emerge during summer—instead of the usual one or two. The excess beetles infect trees, causing more of the trees to die. And the dead trees create a fire hazard.

graph that showed the changes in Earth's carbon dioxide concentrations, now known as the Keeling Curve. The curve plots the global rise of carbon dioxide in the atmosphere since 1958. It shows an increase of 21 percent from 1958 to 2006 and an increase of more than 35 percent since before the Industrial Revolution.

With Keeling and Revelle's work, global warming became a topic of serious concern among climatologists. Scientists realized just how fast carbon dioxide levels were increasing. For the first time, the scientific community began to understand the warming would have a serious, negative impact on Earth.

A New Greenhouse Gas

In the 1970s, scientists began to notice that chemicals called chlorofluorocarbons (CFCs) were being added to the environment in increasing amounts. CFCs were used in the cooling systems of air conditioners and refrigerators. They were also used to make plastic foam and aerosol spray bottles. Scientists linked CFCs to global warming. Researchers also began to suspect that CFCs were eating away Earth's ozone layer—the atmospheric layer that absorbs much of the sun's harmful ultraviolet rays.

In 1987, more than 24 countries, including the

United States, signed the Montreal Protocol, agreeing to ban CFCs. By the early 2000s, 189 countries had signed the protocol. Manufacturers in these countries are replacing CFCs in refrigerators, air conditioners, and aerosol spray bottles with other chemicals. Unfortunately, many of these replacement chemicals also have been found to contribute to global warming.

THE INTERGOVERNMENTAL PANEL ON CLIMATE CHANGE

The Intergovernmental Panel on Climate Change (IPCC) involves more than 2,500 leading scientists and economists from around the world. Their mission is to assess climate change and its possible effects, and to offer solutions. In 1990, the IPCC released its first report, noting that increasing coal and oil use would make global warming even worse. It stated that to bring climate change under control, the world would have to reduce its carbon dioxide emissions by more

Thomas Midgely Jr.

When Thomas Midgely Jr. invented chemicals called chlorofluorocarbons (CFCs) in the 1930s, the world rejoiced. These chemicals were first used to refrigerate food and later in air conditioning for homes and businesses.

Midgely invented Freon 12—a trademark name used for several CFCs—in 1931 while he was working in the General Motors Frigidaire Division. Of course, when Midgely invented the substance, he did not know that CFCs would destroy large sections of the ozone layer—the protective layer in Earth's atmosphere that shields the planet from the sun's harmful ultraviolet radiation. In 1987, the Montreal Protocol banned CFCs.

Global Warming and Coral Reefs

According to a 2005 study, warming of the Indian Ocean has killed off many coral reefs, which has in turn reduced the varieties of fish in the area. When water temperatures rise, coral colonies eject algae and turn white—a process called bleaching. Bleaching kills the coral and the life that depends on the coral. Many scientists blame global warming for a reduction in coral reefs worldwide.

"Bleaching is a global issue, and it's driven by global warming," said Nicholas Graham, the lead author of the study and a tropical marine biologist. "So the onus is on all of us, really. We need to reduce greenhouse gases and take these issues seriously."[1]

than 60 percent below what emissions were in 1990.

The IPCC has since released reports describing the scientific evidence that human activities are largely responsible for global warming. A 2007 IPCC report predicted that if greenhouse gases are not cut back soon, the world will see more water shortages, health epidemics, crop failures, and other disasters.

In 1992, the United Nations Framework Convention on Climate Change international treaty committed signing countries to a long-term goal of controlling global warming quickly enough to avoid dangerous climate change. More than 190 countries, including the United States, have signed and ratified this treaty. This inspired the 1997 Kyoto Protocol.

Warmer ocean waters can kill coral reefs and the fish that depend on the reefs.

Seasonal melting of Greenland's ice sheet

STUDYING GLOBAL WARMING

To assess global warming, scientists look at the history of Earth's temperatures going back thousands of years. But how do they acquire this data from periods before people recorded temperatures?

They use a variety of methods, one of which is to study ice. Since the 1980s, scientists have been cutting into ice in Greenland and Antarctica. Researchers study the ice layers as well as the air bubbles that date back hundreds of thousands of years. This method allows scientists to study past ice ages. The air pockets contain carbon dioxide. By measuring this carbon dioxide, scientists can deduce what the composition of the atmosphere was. By examining the makeup of the ice layers, they can determine the global temperature at any given time in history. This research has shown that the level of carbon dioxide in Earth's atmosphere has increased 35 percent since the mid-1800s.

The other major question researchers face is: How much hotter will it get? The answer depends on two main factors. One factor, the continued rate of greenhouse gases, is under human control. The other has to do with how the climate responds to greenhouse gases. For example: How much will ice caps melt, causing further heating? Will plant life increase, helping to reduce greenhouse gases?

If greenhouse gas emissions continue to rise, the world could see an increase in 4.3 to 11.5 degrees Fahrenheit (2.4° to 6.4° C) by 2100. In a scenario where emissions increase slowly and then fall after

2050, increased warming by 2100 could range from 1.9 to 5.2 degrees Fahrenheit (1.2° to 2.9° C).

Recording Ancient Climates

In addition to ice samples, scientists study:

• *Sea sediment.* Scientists evaluate layers of sediment at the bottom of the ocean floor. During cold periods, less ice melts. Therefore, ocean currents are weaker and carry smaller bits of sediment. During periods of warming, ice melts faster, creating stronger currents and carrying larger sediment grains.

• *Fossilized pollen.* Declining amounts of fossilized pollen indicate that there was less vegetation during a given time period. Typically, this means less rainfall and colder temperatures. For instance, scientists in Peru found increased pollen in a 4,000-year-old core from a lakebed. Those findings indicated warmer temperatures after the year 900, which coincided with what is known as the Medieval Warming Period. During the Little Ice Age (around 1600–1850), the researchers found that the fossilized pollen declined. By looking at the types of pollen, scientists can identify species that lived in different climates. That offers more clues about temperatures in different periods.

• *Tree rings.* Wider tree rings mean that a tree grew under better conditions indicated by warmer weather and greater rainfall. During cold and dry periods, tree rings are smaller. A tree does not need to be alive for scientists to accurately determine weather conditions when it was alive.

Scientists use the computerized climate model to address climate change. Climate models have become a topic of some debate. A difference in just a fraction of a degree can have a major impact on Earth. Policymakers need accurate predictions in order to assess global warming and take appropriate action.

Using Climate Models

Actually constructing a

climate model involves entering various forms of data
into a computer to calculate complicated formulas and
equations. Some of the data that typically would be
accounted for in a climate model are surface
temperatures, ocean currents, cloud formations, plant
cover, wind speed and direction, and the expected
increase or decrease in greenhouse gases. All these data
are programmed into computers, which then calculate
the climate effects on square plots of land. These plots
of land represent the surface area of Earth. The model
can be constructed to make these square plots small or
large. A smaller square will give scientists a more
accurate portrayal, but they require many more
calculations.

Scientists also use models to calculate what the
climate was like in the past. Indeed, this is how scientists
know that the models have a good chance of being
accurate. Scientists have compared data the models
produce for a given period to actual data that is
available.

Climate models and their results are still subject to
some uncertainties. Scientists do not fully understand
all the climate processes that operate in the atmosphere,
ocean, and land. For instance, cloud formation is one
area of uncertainty because it happens on such a local

A Financial Boon in Colorado?

Could global warming benefit ski resorts in Colorado? According to some scientists, global warming would push the snowline up higher on mountains and perhaps make the skiing season shorter. This may sound harmful to Colorado's high-altitude ski resorts. However, ski resorts at lower altitudes would probably be hurt even more. With their competition reduced, Colorado ski resorts could be in store for a financial windfall.

A study conducted in Scotland predicted that ski vacations in the European Alps might end by 2030. However, it stated American resorts at higher altitudes, including Colorado's Breckenridge, Vail, and Aspen resorts, would be able to stay open much longer. Those resorts "could find Europeans flocking to their slopes as the global climate changes," the study stated.[1]

level. Scientists are not sure how increasing temperatures will affect cloud formation or how cloud formation will affect temperatures. As a result, they have to speculate on how best to reproduce this process in climate models. Also, scientists currently can only speculate on how different organisms may react to global warming. Plants could slow global warming by absorbing more carbon dioxide. Other factors such as deforestation, the emission of greenhouse gases and aerosols, the erosion of rocks, and changes in marine life could interact in various and complex ways.

An Improved Climate Model

As time goes by, climate models are becoming more complex and more accurate. Noah S. Diffenbaugh, a climatologist at Purdue University, was among those who worked on a climate model in 2005. At the time, the model was the most comprehensive of any to make predictions about the continental United States during the next century.

The advanced model was able to account for factors that past models neglected, such as how snow reflects sunlight back into space and how mountain ranges block weather fronts from traveling to more distant areas.

Purdue scientists were able to make predictions for squares of land that were only 15 miles (25 km) wide as opposed to the usual 30 miles (50 km) wide. Among the model's findings were:

❖ The Southwest will experience even more heat waves and less rain.

❖ The Gulf Coast will become hotter. It will receive more rain over shorter time frames. The net result will be more rain, but it will not be steady. There will be longer dry spells.

❖ In the Northeast, summers will be longer and hotter. "Imagine the weather during the hottest two weeks

Early Spring in the Arctic

Data already show that spring in the Arctic is arriving two weeks earlier. Toke Hoye and his colleagues at the University of Copenhagen in Denmark observed signals of spring two weeks earlier in 2005 compared with 1996. For instance, they saw plants flowering sooner and insects and spiders emerging earlier from hibernation.

"In the short term, this is probably mainly good news, since the growing season is extending and the organisms now have more time to complete their reproductive cycle," Hoye said. But he added that over the long term, the news is not as good. "Competition from these species is likely to push [other] species toward the north with the risk of extinction."[2]

of the year," Diffenbaugh said. "The area could experience temperatures in that range lasting for periods of up to two months by century's end."[3]

❖ Overall, the continental United States will become warmer, and winter will become shorter.

Diffenbaugh had harsh words for those who question the validity of models. "The more detail we look at with these models, the more dramatic the climate's response is," he said. He took issue with critics who have complained that climate models cannot be trusted because they lack "spatial detail." These critics say that the size of the square of land that is being studied is too large. Diffenbaugh went on,

> In terms of looking at the whole contiguous United States, we've quadrupled the spatial detail and, as a result, it appears that climate change is going to be even more dramatic than we previously thought. Of course, we can never be completely certain of the future, but it's clear that as we consider more and more detail, the picture of future climate change becomes more and more severe.[4]

*Longer, hotter summers in the continental United States
could affect crops and growing cycles.*

The impact of global warming on polar bear habitats concerns scientists.

THE IMPACT ON LIFE
ON EARTH

Warming is already affecting plants and animals. It is changing many species' lifecycles and habitats. But questions still remain: What is the extent of global warming's impact on plants and animals? How quickly will it cause extinctions? How will global warming affect humans? The answers depend largely on how quickly global warming progresses—which, in turn, depends on what measures are taken to counteract it.

HABITATS ARE HARMED

Warmer temperatures have caused many species to flee their normal habitats and move to other areas that are less suited for their survival.

The polar bear provides an example of how global warming may affect a habitat. Polar bears in the Arctic stand on large chunks of ice as they hunt fish, seals, and other sea life. Recently, several dead polar bears have been found floating along the Alaskan Arctic coastline. Some people speculate that the bears are dying from exhaustion trying to find ice to rest on. The ice is melting because of global warming. Others note that there simply is not as much ice available from which the polar bears

Too Many Males

The lizard-like tuatara of New Zealand is the last type of reptile that lived during the dinosaur age some 200 million years ago. According to some scientists, it may soon be extinct because of global warming. Tuataras lay their eggs in the soil, and the warmth of the soil determines the sex of the hatchling. Warmer soil produces males, and colder soil produces females. If males outnumber females in large enough numbers, that could inhibit reproduction, and the species could eventually die off. Male tuataras in one area of New Zealand already outnumber females almost two to one. A four-year breeding process could make it hard for the reptile to adapt, scientists add.

Sea turtles lose nesting areas on Caribbean beaches due to climate changes.

can hunt. If polar bears are unable to change the way they hunt, it will become increasingly difficult, if not impossible, for them to feed.

Scientists are also studying how global warming has disrupted migration and hibernation patterns—processes that hinge on the weather. Some birds, such as the little egret, no longer migrate as far south as they once did. Others, such as the chiff-chaff, now remain in one location throughout the year. Over the next century, scientists expect a loss of one-third of the beaches in the Caribbean that are used by nesting sea turtles. Changing migration and nesting patterns mean these animals also need to find new ways to feed.

By unbalancing ecosystems, global warming affects an area's food chain. Slight changes in ocean temperatures can kill off different levels of plankton on which certain fish feed. If these fish die, marine life such as seals and polar bears also lose their food source. Seals, polar bears, birds, insects, and other organisms then might have to migrate longer distances or at a different time to find other food. It is hard to predict how much of an effect global warming has on migration patterns, but some scientists theorize it could have serious consequences. If the animals cannot find another food source, or if they migrate to an area to which they cannot adapt, the animals may face extinction.

According to one report, 16,119 animal and plant species are in danger of extinction, and species extinction is happening faster than ever before.

An Arctic Tale

An Arctic Tale tells the story of a polar bear cub named Nanu and a female walrus calf named Seela. In the animated film, the animals (who are composite characters of real animals) battle problems that have been exacerbated because of global warming. For example, Seela's herd and Nanu's family must contend with shrinking ice floes and face difficulty finding food. Both the walruses and polar bears end up settling on a rock island, where the walruses become prey to their bear brethren.

"There was a time where we were discussing, should we address climate change or shouldn't we, and we felt a responsibility," said Adam Ravetch, the film's co-director. The movie is narrated by singer-actress Queen Latifah and was produced by National Geographic Films.[1]

Many scientists claim that global warming is a significant contributing cause to this environmental crisis.

Does Warming Cause an Increase in the Cat Population?

Perhaps one of the stranger things global warming has been blamed for is a population explosion among cats. A coalition of animal shelters listed global warming as one of the causes for a "dramatic" increase in the number of cats.

"Many believe global warming is extending cat breeding seasons," said Kathy Warnick, president of Pets Across America. "Cats are typically warm-weather, springtime breeders. However, states that typically experience primarily longer and colder winters are now seeing shorter, warmer winters, leading to year-round breeding."[2] Warnick added that many people now bring boxes of kittens to animal shelters in the winter.

Kelli Ferris, a professor of veterinary medicine, is skeptical. She said,

The increase in the numbers of homeless friendly and feral cats in many parts of the country involves so many factors that I think it would be extremely difficult to quantitatively evaluate the contribution of subtle changes in the environment.[3]

CAN LIFE ADAPT?

Scientists disagree on the dangers that temperature increases pose to organisms. Many plants and animals can be amazingly resilient. For example, research has shown that several Arctic plants have been able to adjust to wide climate changes. In one instance, Arctic plant species repeatedly recolonized a series of remote islands near Norway during 20,000 years of warm and cool temperatures.

Norwegian and French scientists analyzed genetic patterns from more than 4,000 samples of nine plant species from the islands. They found evidence that plant communities were reestablished repeatedly from plant fragments from Russia, Greenland, and other Arctic regions hundreds of miles away.

Throughout history, the evolutionary process has allowed animals to change and adapt to new climates. This occurs through migration and breeding patterns. However, the current rate of climate change is so rapid that many animals may not be able to adapt. Some scientists have predicted that 30 to 40 percent of the species on Earth could be at risk for extinction with warming above another 2 to 5 degrees Fahrenheit (1° to 2° C).

Harm to Humans

Humans are already being affected by global warming. Scientists are certain that higher temperatures in heavily populated areas, such as the Asia-Pacific region, are contributing to the loss of human life. Annually, nearly 80,000 deaths in that area are directly or indirectly tied to changes in the climate. Shigeru Omi, Western Pacific Director of the World Health Organization (WHO), noted that global

A World of Refugees?

Generally, refugees are defined as people who leave their homeland in order to escape persecution or war. As of 2007, there were an estimated 10 million refugees and 25 million internally displaced people (those who have the same status as refugees but lack international protection). Some groups warn that global warming could displace millions more. Climate change, rising sea levels, deforestation, and increasing deserts could all cause people to be displaced.

According to Michele Klein Solomon of the International Organization of Migration, "All around the world, predictable patterns are going to result in very long-term and very immediate changes in the ability of people to earn their livelihoods."[5]

warming "will pose an even greater threat to mankind in the coming decades if we fail to act now."[4]

How do higher temperatures harm humans? Heat waves kill directly. Also, heat contributes to more smog formation and decreased air quality, which can cause asthma-related deaths. The higher temperatures mean droughts, which could decrease crop yields and potentially lead to a shortage of food. In coastal areas, rising water from the temperature increase could cause flooding that would lead to destruction of property, loss of land, and contamination of fresh water supplies. Some areas could experience more frequent and intense hurricanes, while dangerous heat waves sweep across other areas. More indirectly, warming could also lead to the spread of disease.

In recent years, some diseases that are carried by insects have spread. Many health officials say global warming is the culprit. They say that warmer weather

allows insects such as mosquitoes and deer ticks to live longer. This enables them to move into areas where people do not have the physical immunity to fight diseases that these insects carry.

Harvard Medical School has a special center for studying how climate change affects human health. In 2005, the center conducted a study that found that global warming and severe weather affect the number of mosquitoes, their habitat, and their ability to spread diseases such as malaria and West Nile virus. Lyme disease is also spreading via deer ticks.

Others suggest, however, that global warming may not be the only, or even primary, factor contributing to the spread of these diseases. As is often the case in the global warming debate, it is difficult to separate the effects of the warming from other factors. According to some, global warming becomes a kind of "catch-all" explanation for all kinds of problems. Such critics argue that larger populations, globalization, and other factors need to be considered more carefully as contributing causes to the spread of disease.

Record Heat Waves

According to The Union of Concerned Scientists, many studies show that over the last ten years in the

Northern Hemisphere, the average high temperatures are the highest over the past 2,000 years. Between 1979 and 2002, approximately 9,000 people in the United States died from excessive exposure to heat.

Recent data from the National Climate Data Center (NCDC) show that there were more than 50 all-time high temperature records in the United States in July 2006 alone. The NCDC also reported that August 2006 was the fourth warmest August on record for both land and ocean temperatures since people began measuring temperatures in 1880.

Some people caution against placing too much focus on heat waves. They point out that several states have reported all-time record lows in the past decade, with no all-time state record highs reported in the same time period. Such skeptics argue that cold is also a threat, as thousands die of cold-related exposure every year. Could global warming reduce cold-related deaths? While that may be the case, the best scientific information shows that increased heat-related deaths will more than offset this benefit.

Dry, cracked reservoir beds in Spain are the result of record heat waves.

A March 2000 flood in Mozambique displaced thousands of people.

Changing Planet,
Changing Climate

In the movie *The Day After Tomorrow*, global warming leads to disaster as it doles out hurricanes, floods, tornadoes, and tidal waves. People agree that this movie is an exaggeration; however, no one knows for certain what the outcome of ongoing global warming could be on Earth's climate.

The issue is complex because global warming causes a series of effects that, in turn, further affect climate change. For example, more carbon dioxide in the atmosphere could increase plant growth. In turn, living green plants pull carbon dioxide out of the air. Also, as Earth rotates, so do the heat and moisture in the atmosphere, changing rain patterns over the entire planet.

EFFECTS OF MELTING GLACIERS

Most scientists agree that as glaciers melt, sea levels will rise. The question is, how much?

Currently Earth is in an interglacial period—a period between colder glacial periods. James Hansen of the NASA Goddard Institute for Space Studies noted,

> *During the warmest interglacial periods the Earth was reasonably similar to today. But if further global warming reaches 2 or 3 degrees Celsius, we will likely see changes that make Earth a different planet than the one we know. The last time it was that warm was ... about three million years ago, when sea level was estimated to have been about 25 meters (80 feet) higher than today.*[1]

Oceans First

In 2005, a study conducted by a group of climate scientists found that 84 percent of the warming on Earth had occurred in the ocean. According to an article in *World Watch*, "Since oceans take a long time to warm up and release energy to the atmosphere, global warming takes a long time to start and a very long time to stop or reverse."[2]

Greenland is the key to whether global warming will cause significant global flooding. Based on data from 1975 to 2000, scientists concluded that Greenland's ice sheet could melt completely during the next 1,000 years. But between 1996 to 2006, the ice sheet's rate of loss more than doubled. The increased melting since 2000 has greatly altered the original prediction. If Greenland's glaciers do completely melt, global sea levels would rise by about 23 feet (7 m). West Antarctic is also vulnerable and could further increase sea levels by 16 feet (5 m).

What will happen if sea levels rise? Some countries can adapt to rising sea levels. Hong Kong and the Netherlands have carefully planned developed areas to protect them from severe storms. But other places, such as New Orleans, have not been prepared for strong storms or rising sea levels. The 2005 disaster in New Orleans can be viewed as a warning to countries that are not prepared for stronger storm systems or rising sea levels. The poorest locations of Asia and Africa are expected to be hit the hardest by these climate changes.

These areas do not have the funding or resources to prepare for such an event.

One of the worst effects of the ice caps melting may not be the unleashed water but exposing land that previously had been under ice. With more land surface and larger oceans, the planet will absorb even more of the sun's energy. This is the opposite of what polar ice can do: reflect the sun's energy.

The Arctic ice cap also plays a key role in cooling the planet. In *An Inconvenient Truth*, Gore writes, "Melting the Arctic could profoundly change the planet's entire climate pattern." Gore equates the

"Global Dimming" and the Nature of Volcanoes

Scientist James Hansen says that the problem of global warming is even bigger than reported. According to his theory of "global dimming," the true effects of global warming are obscured. Pollution in Earth's atmosphere—and ash from volcanic eruptions—has actually had a cooling effect on the planet. The pollution blocks out sunlight, thereby lowering temperatures. Air pollution covers up the true warming effect of the greenhouse gases. As pollution becomes more controlled, Earth is going to feel much warmer.

Scientists had a chance to test their theory that volcanic eruptions actually contribute to global cooling. In June 1991, Mount Pinatubo, in the Philippines, ejected an enormous amount of dust and sulfur dioxide into the air. It surged 12 miles (19 km) into the atmosphere. The dust spread throughout the world, and the amount of radiation from the sun that reached the troposphere fell 2 percent, confirming scientists' theories about volcanic eruptions.

Data gathering off the central Oregon coast to trace the effects of global warming

world's climate to an engine that redistributes heat from the equator and the tropics to the poles. This redistribution of heat drives wind and ocean currents such as the Gulf Stream and the jet stream, which have followed much the same patterns for thousands of years. "Disrupting them would have incalculable consequences for all of civilization," Gore says.[3]

If these changes do take place, millions of people would be displaced by rising floodwaters. Water-borne diseases would increase. Also, there would be an increase in severe storms in parts of the world. Other

areas would experience drought, causing famine and
other problems. Rising temperatures could cause more
deadly heat waves and kill much of the ocean life that
many communities rely on for food.

CHANGING WEATHER PATTERNS

Jet streams are powerful air currents
that circle the globe in predictable
paths. During the past 27 years,
Earth's jet streams have moved about
70 miles (113 km) closer to the poles.
One of the causes for this shift may be
an increased surface temperature on
Earth. When jet streams flow
differently, it affects weather patterns.
Some areas may experience longer or
more intense droughts, while others
see unexpected rain. Water holes may
dry up, or fields may flood. Such
changes in weather patterns change
ecosystems. They also directly affect
farmers who have tailored their
agricultural practices to the climate.
When the climate changes
unexpectedly, crop yields are affected.

China's Growing Deserts

Deserts now cover one-third of China and continue to grow. While scientists blame most of the problem on practices such as overgrazing and deforestation, they also say that global warming will worsen the situation. As glaciers on the Tibetan Plateau melt, lakes and rivers will be deprived of an essential source of water, which could lead to expanding deserts. The desertification is already affecting grain output in China. According to Lester Brown, president of the Earth Policy Institute, desertification caused grain production to fall approximately 10 percent between 1998 and 2006.

Workers cut silt from the river bed of the receding Ganges River in India.

As the north and south jet streams have moved away from each other and closer to the poles, the tropic and sub-tropic areas around the equator have widened. This means warmer weather in a broader "belt" around the planet. The warmer air can hold more moisture, which can bring out a number of consequences. For example, as warm air moves across wet soil, the air can absorb moisture from the ground. This dries out the soil, which, in turn, can contribute to desertification, or increasing deserts. The warm, humid air then moves elsewhere and dumps heavier-than-normal rains, causing flooding. A similar evaporation process occurs over the ocean, leading to more and stronger hurricanes.

Since global warming can cause strange weather patterns, many people fear a return to the "Dust Bowl" that the United States faced during most of the 1930s. During this time, severe drought contributed to turning much of the central United States into desert. This forced farming families to move elsewhere in search of water and work. Critics argue that not all weather phenomena can be attributed to increasing temperatures. The past has also seen some severe drought in the Great Plains of North America—with or without global warming.

Regardless of strange weather patterns, conservation and prevention efforts are being made in many places.

India's Endangered River

India's Ganges River is holy to approximately 800 million Hindus and provides water to approximately 500 million people. The Gangotri glacier provides most of the river's water in dry months. However, it is melting at a rate of 40 yards (36.6 m) per year. That is twice as fast as the glacier was melting just 20 years ago.

"This may be the first place on Earth where global warming could hurt our very religion," said Veer Bhadra Mishra, director of the Sankat Mochan Foundation, a group that is seeking to preserve the Ganges. "The melting glaciers are a terrible thing. We have to ask ourselves, who are the custodians of our culture if we can't even help our beloved Ganga?"[4]

People are taking measures to limit their production of greenhouse gases. New farming methods are being used to protect topsoil. Oceanside cities are preparing for more damaging storms. Some of these actions are preventative, while others attempt to reverse global warming trends or help people to prepare to live with the effects of the changed climates. ⌒

A Florida beach after Tropical Storm Ernesto

Greenhouse gas emissions from automobiles have inspired research for alternative energy sources.

WAYS TO LIMIT
GREENHOUSE GASES

here are two main ways to limit greenhouse gases: by reducing use of fossil fuels or by keeping the gases out of the atmosphere. To reduce use of fossil fuels, society could switch to alternative energy sources or reduce its total energy use. Greenhouse gases are kept out of the atmosphere either by being trapped underground or stored in living plants.

ALTERNATIVE ENERGY SOURCES

Currently, the world is powered almost exclusively by fossil fuels, most notably petroleum and coal. Fossil fuels pose two main problems: They are running out, and they emit greenhouse gases. Environmentalists hope for a world powered by alternative energy sources, such as wind or sunlight. These energy sources do not emit greenhouse gases and will not run out. However, as many argue, renewable energy comes with its own set of problems. It may not always be practical or reliable. And, because the technology is not developed, it is often more expensive than fossil fuels. Proponents of alternative energy counter that its costs will decrease as the technology is developed.

Cow Dung Could Become a Popular Fuel

American Electric Power Co. (AEP), a utility company that produces more carbon dioxide than any other firm in the United States, believes it can use cow dung to lower the emissions of the gas.

According to the International Energy Agency, methane accounts for 16 percent of worldwide greenhouse gas emissions. Carbon dioxide accounts for 75 percent of such emissions. However, while there is less methane in the atmosphere, it is actually 21 times more powerful a greenhouse gas than carbon dioxide.

AEP is investigating the possibility of covering lagoons filled with livestock waste with plastic tarps. This would trap methane before it enters the air. The methane could then be burned, releasing carbon dioxide, which is not as bad for the atmosphere.

Some see a future in nuclear energy. Like alternative energy, nuclear energy does not emit greenhouse gases. Opponents of nuclear energy contend that this technology is too expensive and unsafe. Nuclear plants make dangerous, radioactive waste that needs to be carefully disposed of and protected. Also, this technology can be used to develop nuclear weapons. They worry that as it spreads, the technology could fall into the wrong hands.

The Cost of Making the Switch

Is it worth it to switch from fossil fuels to alternative energy sources? The answer is complicated. The economic consequences of global warming will occur over decades and centuries. Many people who agree that global warming is harmful to the world's economy sometimes disagree on whether countries should seriously alter their behavior to prevent it. The financial cost of reducing carbon emissions could be tremendous.

A 2006 report issued by the British Treasury assessed the costs and risks associated with switching from fossil fuels to other forms of energy. It estimated that the switch would cost 1 percent of the world's gross domestic product (the market value of all goods sold)

Energy Type	Description	Drawbacks
Wind	Large wind turbines collect energy from the wind. The machines' blades are connected to devices that turn a generator to produce electricity.	Requires back-up power since wind is not always blowing; turbines require a lot of land.
Geothermal Energy	Tubes route steam and hot water from underground hot springs to a plant where the steam turns a generator to make electricity.	Requires hot springs nearby; energy source is site-specific.
Dams	Water flows through the dam and spins turbine blades that are connected to generators. In turn, the generators produce electricity, which is carried along wires to homes and businesses.	Depends on a nearby source of water; structures may destroy habitat for fish and wildlife and submerge valuable land.
Ocean Energy	Waves are directed into a narrow channel that increases their size and power; waves used to spin turbines to generate electricity.	Site-specific.
Solar Energy	Solar panels convert sunlight in solar energy that can be used to heat homes or provide power for any number of devices.	Requires expensive equipment to collect and concentrate sun's energy; interrupted by darkness and cloudy weather.
Hydrogen Fuel Cells	Hydrogen gas and air chemically react to produce electricity in battery-like apparatus.	Expensive.
Biomass	Biomass (leftover organic material, such as wood, manure, and kitchen scraps) can be burned to release heat, or it can be converted into other fuels.	Some methods contribute to air pollution, while others are not energy-efficient.

Alternative energy sources and drawbacks

each year until 2050. The United States' yearly share of the cost would be less than the cost of the Iraq war and comparable to the money spent to boost antiterrorism activities after the September 11, 2001, attacks.

The report describes a range of possible outcomes from the switch. The economy could actually be bolstered if industry were to stop using fossil fuels. Savings in energy costs could offset the expense involved in making such a transition. The report goes on to say, however, that such a transition could also be more expensive than expected and may lead to a decrease in productivity.

The report concludes that a loss of productivity is well worth the risk. "The demands of strong, early action on climate change outweigh the costs," it reads.[1] According to Nicholas Stern, the report's author,

> *Our actions over the coming few decades could create risks of major disruption to economic and social activity, later in this century and in the next, on a scale similar to those associated with the great wars and the economic depression of the first half of the 20th Century.*[2]

INTERNATIONAL COMPETITION IS A FACTOR

What if U.S.-based companies made the huge investment necessary to virtually eliminate the production of greenhouse gases, and other countries did not? Global warming would still continue. Many also worry that this would put the United States at a competitive disadvantage in the global economy. The costs of production for various products would increase, U.S. products would be more expensive, and trade imbalances —the difference in exports and imports between countries—would worsen. Such consequences could lead to U.S. companies moving overseas, where fossil fuels were still in use. In this scenario, thousands of people would lose their jobs. Indeed,

Alternative Energy Already Big Business

What might be in store for the future of the alternative energy business? According to the UN Environment Programme (UNEP), $100 billion was spent on alternative energy and energy efficiency programs worldwide in 2006. This is a 25 percent increase compared to just one year earlier. According to Executive Director Achim Steiner,

One of the new and fundamental messages of this report is that renewable [or, alternative] energies are no longer subject to the vagaries of rising and falling oil prices—they are becoming generating systems of choice for increasing numbers of power companies, communities and countries irrespective of the costs of fossil fuels. The other key message is that this is no longer an industry solely dominated by developed country industries. Close to 10 percent of investments are in China with around a fifth in total in the developing world. We will need many sustained steps towards the de-carbonizing of the global economy. It is clear that in respect to renewables those steps are getting under way.[3]

Dell, a computer maker, has joined the fight against global warming. Dell recently introduced its "Plant a Tree for Me Campaign," which it launched in partnership with The Conservation Fund and Carbonfund.org. Because of photosynthesis, trees and other green plants reduce the amount of carbon dioxide in the air. Visitors to Dell's Web site can make a donation to plant a tree in order to offset the carbon dioxide emitted by personal computers and other information technology products. According to Dell's Web site, an American citizen can offset the yearly carbon-dioxide emissions associated with his or her use of information technology products by donating $99 to the program. Dell's partners use 100 percent of the donations to plant trees.

the entire U.S. economy could be ruined.

Others, however, point out that this has not been proven to be the case. For instance, regulations in Europe and Japan regarding carbon emissions are more strict than U.S. regulations, and yet they have trade surpluses (exporting more than they import). Moreover, if the world as a whole becomes more concerned about the environment, there could even be a backlash against countries that are not environmentally friendly. In this scenario, it is the countries that do not address global warming that face economic risk.

What You Can Do

Alternative energy does not emit greenhouse gases, but it is not widely available. Until it is, environmentalists urge individuals to conserve, or cut back on, their energy use. How can this be done? As the

Environmental Protection Agency (EPA) points out, driving cars and using electricity is not wrong. People just need to be smart about it.

PLANT TREES

One of the main factors contributing to global warming has been the loss of forests. Forests are being cleared to make way for farms, pastures, and housing developments, and few forests are being planted in their place. This process, called deforestation, contributes to global warming in two ways. First, green plants take carbon dioxide out of the atmosphere through their leaves. So as the planet loses its trees, it also loses its ability to cope with increasing greenhouse gases. Second, after the trees are cut down, they are burned. This releases the carbon that was stored inside the plant back into the atmosphere.

One way to reduce greenhouse gases, then, is to reduce deforestation while planting new trees. This solution may sound simple, but it does have practical problems. In many cases, open land for planting trees is just not available. Meanwhile the demands of international business and agriculture require more and more clearing of land. Also, in order to affect change, trees would need to be planted on a massive, international scale. This would take much planning and cooperation between governments, which, as has been shown with the Kyoto Protocol, is a difficult feat.

STORING CARBON UNDERGROUND

In Norway, an oil company is making money not only by selling the fossil fuel, but also by combating the fuel's negative effects. This is the only company in the world that is turning a profit by making use of a new technology. The technology allows the company to trap and store greenhouse gas emissions underground before they ever reach the atmosphere.

Reward: $25 Million

A British millionaire has contributed his own innovative solution to reducing global warming. Entrepreneur Richard Branson thinks technology may provide the answer to the problem and has come up with a way to inspire inventors everywhere. Branson is offering a $25 million prize to anyone who can come up with a device that can remove carbon dioxide from the atmosphere.

For decades, oil companies have been injecting carbon dioxide into oil wells as a way to increase oil production. Now other companies, such as a coal-burning power plant, can imitate this practice as a way to fight global warming. The practice, called carbon capture, "has the potential to reduce more than 90 percent of an individual plant's carbon emissions," according to Lynn Orr, director of the Global Climate and Energy Project.[4] Considering that power plants contribute 40 percent of the world's harmful greenhouse gases, that could mean a significant savings in emissions worldwide. Supporters are optimistic about its uses in China and other developing nations. Carbon capture offers those countries the opportunity to develop using fossil fuels and minimize the negative effects.

Skeptics of carbon capture identify a number of concerns. Will the stored carbon leak? Experts say that leaks, if any, would be slow. In that case, the stored carbon could contaminate drinking water, which often comes from groundwater. The bigger issue, perhaps, is whether this technology will slow the development of alternative energy sources. Will it strengthen the world's reliance on fossil fuels? After all, carbon capture is limited in scope. It does not address automobiles, which are a major contributor to global warming.

Energy-Saving Ideas

Many organizations offer the following tips to reduce the use of fossil fuels:

• Use less energy by carpooling, taking the bus, riding a bike, or walking.

• Save electricity by turning off lights and other electrical appliances when not in use. Most often, when people use electricity, more greenhouse gases enter the air.

• Buy energy-saving products such as compact flourescent lightbulbs, which last longer and use less energy.

• Recycle. This sends less trash to the landfill, saving natural resources such as trees and oil.

• Buy recycled products such as napkins or trash bags. Look for three arrows that make a circle.

• Urge your parents to buy an energy efficient car, instead of the biggest or fastest car. Hybrid vehicles use less fuel, and therefore emit less carbon dioxide.

These may seem like small things, but when thousands of people participate, such measures do make a difference.

Mark Zoback, a scientist who researches the technology, says these concerns are valid. However, carbon capture "is only a bridge technology," he says.

> *Maybe we have another hundred years of using fossil fuels, and then we'll be on to better and smarter things, one hopes. If we're going to be creating greenhouse gases for another hundred years, it's a huge problem right now.... Nonetheless, our dependence on fossil fuels is not going to last forever.*[5]

Oil pumps in Wyoming

In Montreal, Canada, protesters call for action against global warming.

POLICYMAKERS BATTLE GLOBAL WARMING

hich countries have caused global warming? Which countries are paying the price? A drought in Africa that will not end has been blamed on global warming. Low-lying areas

around the world are at risk from the threat of rising sea levels. Some people think countries such as the United States should help poorer countries that may not have the technology or money to do anything about global warming. These groups point out that wealthier countries are responsible for a large part of the greenhouse gases in the atmosphere. Others disagree that wealthier countries have a responsibility to help other countries. So what are different countries doing about global warming?

The first report of the International Panel on Climate Change (IPCC), in 1990, stated global warming was a real issue and that countries should take action. In 1992, governments created the United Nations Framework Convention on Climate Change (UNFCCC). This convention outlined how countries could deal with global warming. The UNFCCC called for nations to stabilize their greenhouse gas concentrations in a manner that continued economic development and protected food production and ecosystems. The UNFCCC outlined long-term goals and did not impose mandatory targets or any penalties for failing to achieve goals. So the UNFCCC led to the 1997 Kyoto Protocol, a binding treaty that set targets for emission reductions as well as deadlines.

Issues Surrounding the Kyoto Protocol

Information from the IPCC reports was taken into consideration in the drafting of the Kyoto Protocol. The protocol's first step to reduce greenhouse gases is to require each country to lower its greenhouse gas emissions by a specific amount. Not every country has the same limits. The total reduction goal for all of the countries is 5 percent below levels of emissions recorded in 1990. The deadline for countries to cut their emissions is 2012. By 2007, 169 countries had approved the agreement. This does not include the United States. President George W. Bush argues that if the United States follows the protocol, too many American workers might lose their jobs. He also believes that developing countries such as China, India, and Brazil should be held to the same standards.

The Kyoto Protocol is controversial because it does not require developing nations to reduce their greenhouse gas emissions. For example, China and India have approved the agreement. They have some of the largest populations in the world and some of the highest levels of emissions. In 2007, China surpassed the United States as the country that emits the largest overall amount of greenhouse gases. However, a distinction needs to be made between total output of

Kenyan Nobel Peace Prize laureate Wangri Maathai speaks at the Kyoto International Conference in 2005.

greenhouse gases and output per person. Per person, China's emissions are still much lower than emission levels in the United States. In other words, a Chinese citizen's individual use of fossil fuels is much lower than the average American's usage.

Those in favor of the Kyoto Protocol argue that developing countries deserve the opportunity to industrialize, just as the United States and Europe did during the last century. Proponents argue that industrialized nations should not require these countries to lower emissions. Instead, the United States and other world leaders should help developing countries industrialize without repeating past mistakes. They look to cleaner energy sources as a way for China and India to industrialize without paying the price in air pollution and global warming.

The protocol allows emissions "trading" among countries. This means that if one country emits less than the allotted amount, it can "sell" credits to countries that exceeded their emissions allowances. Countries can also earn credits through projects that lower emissions. So far, it has been a difficult task tracking what each country is doing. Different nations use different reporting systems, and some, such as the United States, do not require data to be verified by a third party. This means businesses could provide inaccurate data that has not been cross-checked. Without uniform reporting standards or measuring tools, emission reports can be very rough estimates.

Fred Pearce, author of an article published in *New Scientist,* wrote,

> *Under Kyoto, each government calculates how much carbon dioxide, methane and nitrous oxide its country emits*

by adding together estimated emissions from individual sources. Now two teams that have monitored concentrations of greenhouse gases in the atmosphere say that they have convincing evidence that the figures reported by many countries are wrong, especially for methane.[1]

Methane does not remain in the atmosphere as long as carbon dioxide, but according to Pearce, its immediate effect—ton for ton—is approximately 100 times greater (and the overall effect is 21 times greater). For example, methane emissions from the United Kingdom and France may be putting the countries over their total emissions limit.

Some people and lawmakers argue that the protocol's demands are too strict and that it is too difficult to comply with. But others say it is not strict enough because the limits it places on member countries are not enough to slow global warming and will have little, if any, effect on global

A Tax on Energy Use?

In 2007, Pennsylvania Governor Ed Rendell sought to push through a controversial bill that would promote less energy use. The bill had an interesting compo-nent: It would place a new tax on energy use, and the money generated from that tax would help pay for alternative energy and conservation efforts.

Many people in Pennsylvania question whether a tax is needed to fund alternative fuel efforts, but Rendell pointed out that 15 states and Washington, D.C., already have such a tax. Rendell said the tax would cost the average customer just five dollars per month. This raises interesting ques-tions about how much people are willing to spend to reduce global warming.

temperatures. Some scientists now want to create a global system for checking countries' emissions claims by directly measuring concentrations of greenhouse gases in the air. The Carbon Tracker, a new tool created by the National Oceanic & Atmospheric Administration (NOAA), may do just that.

THE PRESIDENT'S APPROACH

President George W. Bush's approach to global warming and energy is controversial. Although Bush has said he is focused on reliable and affordable energy

---

President George W. Bush

Many environmental activists have criticized President George W. Bush for not urging the United States to adhere to the Kyoto Protocol and for failing to lessen greenhouse gas emissions. But during his presidency, Bush's views about global warming have changed. In July 2005, he said that human activities were contributing to global warming. In 2007, he mentioned global warming in his State of the Union Address.

Later in the year, Bush delivered a speech proposing the United States establish a "long-term global goal" for cutting greenhouse gas emissions.[2] He said he planned to meet with 10 to 15 other countries that produce large amounts of greenhouse gases to try to establish targets for reducing emissions over the next 10 to 20 years.

Other world leaders applauded Bush for speaking out about global warming. Angela Merkel, chancellor of Germany and president of the European Union, said, "What is positive is that we can see from the speech that the president made earlier today that nobody can ignore the question of climate change."[3]

that is good for the environment, many people are critical of his record on the environment and, particularly, his opposition to the Kyoto Protocol.

Among them is Kurt Gottfried, a physics professor at Cornell University and chairman of the Union of Concerned Scientists. Gottfried believes relations between scientists and the government historically have been good in the United States. However, in recent years there has been a lot of friction. Gottfried said,

> *The best known example was when the White House tried to prevent scientific information about the possible impact of climate change from appearing in an important report that was about to be published by the Environmental Protection Agency.*[4]

That led to a protest in February 2004 involving more than 50 scientists, including many who had won Nobel Prizes for their work and some who had been advisers to former presidents.

Since the president and lawmakers have not yet approved the Kyoto Protocol, many state and local officials are adopting their own policies to reduce emissions. One approach has been to demand that

States Fight Global Warming

As global warming becomes more pressing, some states are not waiting for the national government to take action. Governor Arnold Schwarzenegger of California recently pushed through legislation that made his state the first in the nation to adopt a statewide cap on greenhouse-gas emissions. Schwarzenegger believes global warming is one of the most critical issues of the twenty-first century.

Governor Charlie Crist of Florida agrees. In June 2007, Crist vetoed an energy bill that would have required the eco-friendly construction of government buildings, more research on alternative fuels, and the monitoring of greenhouse gas emissions. The reason he vetoed the bill, he said, was because it did not go far enough.

While some people laud states for addressing global warming, others fear that widely differing laws could make it difficult to do business in the United States.

utility companies use alternative energy resources to generate energy. California has been a leader in the fight against global warming. The state has committed to cutting greenhouse gas emissions to 80 percent below 1990 levels by 2050. To that end, the state has passed legislation requiring that automakers reduce their vehicles' carbon dioxide emissions 30 percent by 2016. Ten other states plan on adopting the same standards if the law survives a court challenge from automakers.

Martin J. Chavez, the mayor of Albuquerque, New Mexico, told the *Washington Post*, "Like most mayors, I'm disappointed the federal government has not taken more of a lead on this issue, but so be it. We're moving forward."[5] Chavez is increasing public transportation in Albuquerque. He and other U.S. mayors have vowed to make their cities carbon-neutral by 2030. While the cities will continue to emit greenhouse gases, they will offset these emissions by investing in projects, such as a wind-power plant or reforestation project, that reduce emissions elsewhere. So net emissions will be zero.

WORLD MEETING

On October 3, 2006, leaders from 20 of the world's most polluting nations met in Mexico to discuss ways of dealing with global warming before the Kyoto Protocol expires in 2012. Countries represented at the meeting included the United States, Canada, France, Germany, Italy, Japan, Russia, the United Kingdom, China, India, and Brazil. British Foreign Secretary Margaret Beckett told the leaders and the Associated Press that it is a myth that effective action on climate change is bad for the economy. She said environmentally friendly technologies would create jobs, not reduce them. Even after another meeting in early 2007, the United States refused to

Western Governors Take Global Warming Seriously

While others debate about global warming, the Western Governors Association is focusing on measures to produce cleaner energy. In June 2007, the governors held a conference in South Dakota to brainstorm ways to reduce greenhouse gas emissions. Western states have a big stake in the debate, as they produce much of the coal and oil that contribute to carbon dioxide emissions. "I think it's clear to anyone who has been at this conference and other conferences that this is the issue of our time," said the group's chairman, Wyoming Governor Dave Freudenthal.[6] The governors discussed several initiatives, such as trapping carbon emissions and storing them underground as well as using solar and wind energy.

sign the Kyoto Protocol.

Because of its unsettled policies on global warming, the United States often finds itself at the center of the debate. While the U.S. government works with other nations to determine the most effective worldwide approach to the problem, many other nations, businesses, and private organizations are already taking action.

British Prime Minister Tony Blair and U.S. President George W. Bush in 2005, during Kyoto Protocol talks

A Greenpeace activist in Montreal calls attention to global warming during a United Nations Climate Change Conference.

WHAT ORGANIZATIONS ARE DOING

oday, hundreds of organizations help the environment, and global warming is very important to them. Most environmental organizations have free newsletters available on the Internet. These organizations are funded mostly by public donations.

Forms of Activism

Environmental organizations protest in a number of ways. Though they do stage demonstrations in person, many also organize what they call a "virtual march." This is an online protest intended to influence policymakers through the power of numbers. Thousands of people add their names to online petitions to show their support of a particular agenda. Those petitions are then sent to politicians.

Other organizations, such as Greenpeace, launch campaigns in which they urge members and people who visit their Web site to take action. Greenpeace encourages members to call their representatives in Congress and influence them how to vote on bills regarding the environment. In 2002, Greenpeace joined in a lawsuit against the U.S. government for funding fossil-fuel projects without taking into consideration the result such activities might have on the environment.

Most environmental organizations encourage people to take a grassroots approach to helping the environment. This means that people do what they can to help the environment where they live. For example, in 2004 Global Green launched a "Green Schools Initiative" in southern California. Under this program, any new K-12 schools built in Southern California will be "green" schools. They will be built so that they do not contribute to global warming and so they have the least possible impact on the surrounding natural area.

"Green schools lessen the impact of building construction on the environment and set an example for future generations that environmental quality is essential to our long-term well being," says Matt Petersen, president of the organization.[1] According to Petersen, green schools are less expensive to run, and they offer a healthier environment for students and teachers. Also, students can learn about the environment in a unique school that can be used as a teaching tool.

ACTIVISM AT SCHOOLS

More than 1,000 schools from kindergartens to universities participated in Focus the Nation, a day of

discussion about climate change. Participating schools invited politicians, scientists, and other professionals to come to their schools to discuss global warming and climate change.

The event's organizer, Eban Goodstein, is a professor of Environmental and Natural Resource Economics at Lewis and Clark College in Portland, Oregon. Focus the Nation is a project of The Green House Network, a nonprofit organization in Portland that is building a national movement to stop global warming.

According to Goodstein, global warming can be stopped only if people urge the U.S. government to change its environmental policies at the state and federal levels. Inviting a U.S. Senator to talk at their school, community group, or church is a good way for students to do this, he says. Goodstein believes that Focus the Nation helped students feel they have a positive impact on the environment because they directly engaged their political leaders in discussion about climate change.

SOME OIL COMPANIES JOIN THE FIGHT

As the public has begun paying greater attention to global warming, corporations have also started to pay

A melting Exxon ice sculpture helps protesters spread the message about the company's environmental policy.

attention to the issue. Some companies have surprised people with their stance.

For instance, ConocoPhillips is the third-largest oil company in the United States. It made headlines when its chairman and chief executive officer acknowledged that fossil fuels are warming Earth. "The science has become quite compelling," James Mulva said in an interview with Businessweek.com.[3]

ConocoPhillips is taking action. On April 10, 2007, the company vowed to spend $22 million to help Iowa State University develop alternative fuels from corn and switch grass. Less than one week later, the company announced a partnership with Tyson Foods, the chicken producer, to make fuel out of animal fat.

BP, another giant oil company, also is addressing the problem. In February 2007, the company opened a Los Angeles "green" gasoline station, which uses solar panels. Former Chief Executive John Browne said that it is time for oil companies to look "beyond petroleum" in their search for profits.[4]

BP and ConocoPhillips differ from oil giant ExxonMobil in their approaches to global warming.

"Exxpose Exxon"

Most environmental activists are strong critics of ExxonMobil because of its views on global warming. To see the extent of their displeasure, visitors can go to www.exxposeexxon.com. The Web site's founders include Defenders of Wildlife, Greenpeace, the Natural Resources Defense Council, the Sierra Club, the U.S. Public Interest Research Group, and the Union of Concerned Scientists.

These groups argue that ExxonMobil could invest in cleaner, alternative energy but it refuses to do so. They blast the company for its continued interest in drilling for oil in the Arctic.

For its part, ExxonMobil says that its position on global warming has been misunderstood. It has recently cut its funding to a number of groups that argue global warming is not a serious problem or not caused by human activities. ExxonMobil also has begun participating in talks sponsored by Resources for the Future, a nonprofit Washington, D.C.-based group that is discussing options on how to regulate the emission of greenhouse gases.

Shopping Habits Have an Impact

Climate Counts is a non-profit organization that has rated 56 consumer companies according to their environmental practices. The group hopes that its ratings can help combat global warming. Climate Counts wants consumers to use the ratings to buy products from companies seeking to address global warming and avoid companies thought to be contributing to the problem.

Among the groups that Climate Counts applauds are Canon, Nike, and IBM. Those with bad reports include Jones Apparel Group, CBS, Burger King, Wendy's, and Amazon.com.

The ratings are not based strictly on the levels of greenhouse gases emitted. Each rating takes into account the company's efforts to reduce emissions, whether it supports legislation that seeks to curb global warming, and whether it clearly discloses its activities.

ExxonMobil has been attacked by environmentalists for its support of groups that say global warming is not caused by human activities. Though the company has stopped funding many of these groups and has softened its stance on global warming, activists are not satisfied. In February 2007, the chief executive of the company told an industry gathering that he doubted burning fossil fuels was causing the ice caps to melt and temperatures to rise.

While many people praise the fact that some oil companies are beginning to take actions against global warming, others are skeptical. Skeptics argue that companies are offering just a small portion of their profits. They argue that oil companies may just be trying to improve their image with the public.

Large oil companies have varying stances on global warming.

Commission euro
Europese Commi

Barroso & climate change: big talk, big emissions.

gas-guzzler. CO₂ emissions: 265 g/km

Friends of
the Earth
urope

Barroso & le climat : pa

Son 4x4 pétrophage. CO₂ émis

Friends of
the Earth
Europe

*In May 2006, protesters rallied outside the European Union Commission
headquarters.*

The Future of Global
Warming

lobal warming raises many questions.
Many of these questions pertain to the
effects of global warming. How will it affect plant and
animal life? Habitats? Ecosystems? The food chain?
Migration patterns? What will be its effects on human

health? How will the climate change from region to region? What will be the cost of increased drought, floods, and storms on agriculture, business, and public health? How will developing countries be affected?

The effects of global warming usually trigger further effects. For example, global warming melts ice caps. This raises sea levels, which endangers seaside communities, which leads to increasing numbers of refugees. Sometimes the effects counteract each other. For example, global warming induces an increase in plant life, which then reduces greenhouse gases. It is no wonder, then, that scientists, policymakers, and average citizens struggle to accurately assess the problem. For that reason, there are so many viewpoints about what should be done.

How can technological solutions, such as alternative energy and carbon capture, be implemented? What are the costs? Whose responsibility is it to pay for reducing global warming? Should developed countries, such as the United States, bear most of the burden because they are responsible for the majority of greenhouse gases? Should developing countries, such as China and India, be responsible for reducing emissions as well? Should the United States sign the Kyoto Protocol? What laws can be made at the national level? At the

The Price of Change

How much is the average American family willing to pay to "solve" global warming? About $21 a month, according to a poll conducted by researchers at the Massachusetts Institute of Technology. How much would it cost each family to implement the changes proposed by the Kyoto Protocol? About $225 a month, according to Wharton Econometric Forecasting Associates. And how much would it cost if global warming goes unsolved? According to the Stern Review issued by the British Treasury, the entire global economy could shrink by as much as 20 percent.

state level? What can you do? Perhaps the most important question is: Can global warming be stopped? Many scientists believe that the damage from carbon dioxide and other gases cannot be completely reversed.

The Best That Can Be Done

Dan Lashof, of the Natural Resources Defense Council's (NRDC) Air and Energy Program, is one such scientist who believes the damage cannot be completely reversed. He said some global warming will continue until humanity greatly decreases the amount of greenhouse gases currently entering the atmosphere. He said that even once this is done, it would probably take several decades for Earth to cool. Some scientists believe it will take even longer. Lashof said, "But once emissions have been cut enough so that the levels of global warming pollutants in the atmosphere stabilize, we can eventually stop human-induced global warming."[1]

Stephen Schneider, a biology professor at Stanford University, points out that one of the biggest challenges in stopping global warming depends on what happens with countries such as China and India that are going through industrial revolutions now. The United States and other countries that were the first to put greenhouse gases into the air need to take the lead in fighting global warming, he added. Wealthy countries should help poorer countries to begin using alternative energies right away.

Schneider agrees that it is already too late to completely reverse the damage caused by global warming. But he said, "The longer we delay in doing something about it right now, the more damaging it's going to be and the more expensive it's going to be to fix."[2] His solution to slowing global warming would be to legally require people to conserve energy and buy more energy-efficient products. He

An Unprecedented Lawsuit

California surprised many in June 2007 when it filed a lawsuit against San Bernardino County, a section of the state. Allegedly, the county failed to account for the emission of greenhouse gases when it updated its 25-year blueprint for growth. According to California's attorney general, county officials did not do enough to reduce sprawl, or poorly planned neighborhoods. Sprawl causes people to drive more, which burns more gasoline and emits more greenhouse gases.

The lawsuit argues that the 1970 California Environmental Quality Act requires that greenhouse gases be regulated like any other pollutant. If California wins its lawsuit, it could force other cities and counties to take steps to limit sprawl, promote compact development, promote mass transit, and require builders to design energy-efficient houses.

also said there should be government fees for pollution from vehicles and factories.

Frances Cairncross, former president of the British Association for the Advancement of Science, said that since global warming cannot be stopped, people must focus on adapting to a warmer world. "We need to … prepare for a hotter, drier world, especially in poorer countries," she said.[3] That might involve developing crops that can handle very hot weather, not building in areas that could get flooded, and constructing more structures to hold back floods.

An Important Senate Debate

While some states are writing their own laws to curb the emissions of greenhouse gases, the national government is becoming more involved. In 2007, senators passed a bill that requires all passenger vehicles to get at least 35 miles (56 km) per gallon by 2020 instead of the current 25 miles (40 km) per gallon.

The legislation, however, was under fierce debate. Critics of the bill said the standards were too high and would have an adverse effect on U.S. automakers. They suggested different rules that would adopt variable standards depending on whether the manufacturers were producing compact cars, sedans, wagons,

The Toyota Prius hybrid is an energy-efficient car that is applauded by activists.

sport-utility vehicles, or other types of vehicles.

Furthermore, some senators were accused of protecting the narrow interests of three major automakers in the United States: General Motors, Ford Motor, and DaimlerChrysler AG's Chrysler Group. "The time has come to speak for the American people— not three car manufacturers that are closing plants and laying off people," said Senate Majority Leader Harry Reid, a Democrat from Nevada.[4]

The bill contained other proposals:

❖ It would promote ways to capture greenhouse gases in underground chambers so they would not contribute to global warming.

❖ It would call for an increase in the usage of renewable fuels, including ethanol. Currently, the United States uses 8.5 billion gallons of ethanol. The legislation would state that 36 billion gallons should be used on a yearly basis by 2022.

❖ It would forbid oil companies from dramatically increasing prices during times of national emergency.

Bolstering vehicle standards is just one way that politicians are trying to reduce global warming.

Public's Stance Is Clear

Politicians are reacting to global warming because their constituents are beginning to pay attention to the issue. Whether this is a short-lived phenomenon that is partly the result of the activism spurred by *An*

"Green" Investing on the Rise

What lies ahead in the fight against global warming? Many experts predict an increase in "green" investing, where investors buy stocks from companies that are environmentally friendly or are fighting global warming. According to Holly Isdale, of the financial firm Lehman Brothers, "There's money to be made [in this new trend], and people want to know how to make it."[5]

Investors should note, however, that mutual funds (companies that buy stocks on behalf of individuals) that buy strictly environmentally friendly companies typically charge higher fees than other funds. Moreover, it is difficult to predict which companies will benefit most from either addressing global warming or from the changes it may produce.

Inconvenient Truth, a fad, or a long-lasting grassroots movement remains to be seen. But one thing is clear: for now, people think global warming is a problem that should be dealt with.

In April 2007, a national poll was conducted by researchers at Stanford University in tandem with the *Washington Post* and ABC News. According to the poll, seven out of ten people believe the government should do something about global warming. When asked what the world's most serious environmental threat is, one-third of respondents listed global warming.

A Tax on Greenhouse Gases?

Paul Anderson, chairman of Duke Energy, thinks global warming is a serious problem that demands decisive action. He is urging the government to tax companies based on the amount of greenhouse gases they produce, a measure that would probably anger most energy and oil companies. "If we approach this rationally, it will not be disruptive to the economy and will not turn the world upside down and will, at the same time, address the problem," he said.[6]

PG&E and other utility companies believe that mandatory federal emissions limits would be preferable to countless state regulations. Some utility companies believe that a uniform national standard would make it easier for them to make investment decisions tied to designing power plants.

According to former vice president Al Gore,

There's a sea change underway in American business. What's different in business audiences in the past year or so is a new and widespread receptivity, a keen awareness, an eagerness on the part of large numbers to find out how they can take a leadership position. And a recognition, too, that there are profits to be made.[7]

The same poll found that 85 percent of Americans believe that global warming is "probably" happening. Previous polls conducted by other groups have resulted in similar findings.

With record–high gasoline prices, high media attention, and polls showing that the public favors taking action against global warming issue, it is clear that global warming will continue to be an important political issue for years to come. ⌐

Historic Site in Danger

British explorer Robert Falcon Scott traveled from New Zealand to Antarctica in the early 1900s. During his exploit, he and his crew built a wooden hut at Cape Evans. According to the World Monument Fund (WMF), the historic site is now in danger of collapsing because of global warming. The WMF reports that the hut's timbers, which were frozen for several decades, are waterlogged and rotting because ice is melting.

Scott and his team of explorers died on their return trip from the South Pole. Thousands of artifacts and items associated with their expedition remain in and around the site. The New Zealand government has said it wants the hut preserved, though such an effort could cost $6.7 million.

Global warming is on the forefront of politics worldwide.

TIMELINE

1700s	1760–1850	1824
People begin using coal for heat and energy.	The Industrial Revolution introduces coal-burning machines and other inventions that begin to warm the planet by releasing too many greenhouse gases into the air.	Joseph Fourier describes Earth as a giant greenhouse with an atmosphere that traps heat from the sun.

1958	1970s	1974
Charles Keeling's and Roger Revelle's research shows that carbon dioxide levels are quickly rising.	Large tracts of forest throughout the world are being cleared, contributing to further increases in carbon dioxide emissions.	Scientists describe how chlorofluorocarbons (CFCs) are being added to the environment in increasing amounts.

Late 1800s

Svante Arrhenius discovers that carbon dioxide in the atmosphere is related to climate.

1908

Henry Ford produces millions of Model Ts that emit carbon dioxide and other gases into the air.

1930s

Guy Callendar researches the link between greehouse gas emissions and industrial activity.

1980s

Scientists cut ice cores in Greenland and the North and South Poles to study carbon dioxide concentrations from the past.

1987

The Montreal Protocol is signed by more than two dozen countries, including the United States, to cut back on CFCs.

1988

The Intergovernmental Panel on Climate Change (IPCC) is created to assess climate change, its possible effects on society, and how to correct the problem.

TIMELINE

1990

The IPCC releases its first report on global warming, advising nations to take action.

1992

The United Nations Framework Convention on Climate Change, an international treaty to reduce global warming, is created.

1997

The Kyoto Protocol sets limits for reducing greenhouse gas emissions.

2005

Hurricane Katrina hits the Gulf Coast of the United States, causing massive destruction.

2006

The United States and other countries are working on developing alternative energy sources to fossil fuels.

2007

China surpasses the United States as the largest emitter of greenhouse gases.

2004

More than 50 scientists protest the United States' lack of action regarding global warming.

2005

The Energy Policy Act is created to promote technologies and practices that reduce greenhouse gases.

2005

A Harvard study finds that global warming may contribute to the rise of insect-borne diseases.

2007

By July, 169 countries had signed the Kyoto Protocol. The United States is not one of them.

ESSENTIAL FACTS

AT ISSUE

Scientists trace the beginnings of increased global warming to the Industrial Revolution, which took place in Europe and North America between 1760 and 1850. The Industrial Revolution created a new way of living that increased reliance on machines and factories.

Global warming is driven by human activity. Burning fossil fuels such as coal, oil, and natural gas and the clear-cutting and burning of forests has caused a major climate change on Earth.

The success of the book and documentary *An Inconvenient Truth* is at least partially responsible for an increased awareness about global warming and has mobilized the public to speak out against the perceived threat.

By using computerized climate models, scientists predict further warming and future climate change. Predictions take into consideration many uncertainties, such as how greenhouse gas emissions will increase or decrease.

Evidence shows polar ice caps are melting, causing sea levels to rise. The scope and effects of the melting are uncertain.

Various organizations are targeting global warming and particular companies that supposedly lobby against efforts to solve the problem.

Various states pass legislation targeting global warming. However, this could make it difficult for businesses that will need to keep up with the laws in different states. Some favor national, uniform laws.

Various forms of alternative energy exist, but people debate whether these could become viable options to fossil fuels. Wind power, for instance, does not emit greenhouse gases, but only works when wind is blowing.

CRITICAL DATES

1824
French philosopher Joseph Fourier described Earth as a giant greenhouse with an atmosphere.

1974
Scientists F. Sherwood Rowland and Mario J. Molina at the University of California, Irvine, wrote a paper that was published in the journal *Nature* that described how CFCs were being added to the environment. Later, CFCs were discovered to be destroying the ozone layer and contributing to global warming.

1997
In Kyoto, Japan, representatives of many countries around the world signed the Kyoto Protocol. This document states that by 2012 industrialized nations should lower their greenhouse gas emissions by an average of 5 percent below 1990 emissions levels.

QUOTES

"Our actions over the coming few decades could create risks of major disruption to economic and social activity, later in this century and in the next, on a scale similar to those associated with the great wars and the economic depression of the first half of the 20th Century."—*British economist Nicholas Stern*

"During the warmest interglacial periods the Earth was reasonably similar to today. But if further global warming reaches 2 or 3 degrees Celsius, we will likely see changes that make Earth a different planet than the one we know. The last time it was that warm was ... about three million years ago, when sea level was estimated to have been about 25 meters (80 feet) higher than today."—*James Hansen, NASA Goddard Institute for Space Studies*

ADDITIONAL RESOURCES

SELECT BIBLIOGRAPHY

Christianson, Gale. *Greenhouse: The 200-Year Story of Global Warming.* New York: Penguin Books, 2000.

Climate Change Kids Site. United States Environmental Protection Agency. 12 July 2004. 12 Sept. 2006 <http://www.epa.gov/globalwarming/kids>.

McCaffrey, Paul, ed. *Global Climate Change (Reference Shelf)*. New York: H.W. Wilson Co., 2006.

"NASA Study Finds World Warmth Edging Ancient Levels." 25 Sept. 2006. Goddard Institute for Space Studies. 29 Sept. 2006 <http://www.giss.nasa.gov/research/news/20060925/>.

FURTHER READING

Gaughen, Shasta, ed. *Global Warming*. San Diego: Greenhaven Press, 2005.

Langholz, Jeffrey, and Kelly Turner. *You Can Prevent Global Warming (and Save Money!)*. Kansas City, MO: Andrews McMeel Publishing, 2003.

Lim, Cheng Puay and Cheng Puay Lim. *Our Warming Planet*. Chicago: Raintree, 2004.

Spence, Christopher. *GLOBAL WARMING: personal solutions for a healthy planet*. New York: Palgrave Macmillan, 2005

Web Links

To learn more about global warming, visit ABDO Publishing Company on the World Wide Web at **www.abdopublishing.com**. Web sites about global warming are featured on our Book Links page. These links are routinely monitored and updated to provide the most current information available.

Places To Visit

The Marian Koshland Science Museum
500 Fifth Street, NW, Washington, DC 20001
202-334-1201 or 888-567-4526
www.koshland-science-museum.org/exhibitgcc/index.jsp
The Marian Koshland Science Museum was opened to the public in April 2004. The museum's interactive exhibits demonstrate findings from the National Academy of Sciences. The museum has an extensive exhibit on global warming.

Glacier National Park
Glacier National Park, P.O. Box 128, West Glacier, MT 59936
406-888-7800
www.nps.gov/glac/contacts.htm
See the last remaining glaciers at the park. Tour the park and see how geological forces shaped the rugged landscape millions of years ago.

GLOSSARY

alternative energy
An energy, such as wind, that can be reproduced in a short period of time and generally does not have a negative effect on the environment.

atmosphere
The air surrounding Earth.

carbon dioxide
A heavy, colorless gas that is the fourth largest component of air; the major greenhouse gas.

Celsius
A temperature scale that has 100 degrees between the freezing point (0° C) and boiling point (100° C) of water.

chlorofluorocarbons (CFCs)
Simple gaseous compounds that are used to cool or clean and are believed to contribute to ozone depletion.

climate
The average weather in a certain place over a period of years.

climate model
A computer-generated example created from numerous data and used by scientists to better understand climate changes.

climatologist
A scientist who studies Earth's climate.

deforestation
The large-scale clearing of trees and other plant life to make way for industry and agriculture.

desertification
The increase in deserts due to human and natural causes that include poor farming practices, overgrazing, and global warming.

developing country
A nation that is undergoing industrial growth or an industrial revolution and has not yet fully modernized.

ecosystem
> A community of plants, animals, and other organisms such as bacteria that depend on each other for survival.

Fahrenheit
> A temperature scale in which 32 degrees is the freezing point and 212 degrees is the boiling point.

fossil fuel
> An organic substance, such as coal or petroleum, formed from another time period that is found under the ground and used as a source of energy.

global warming
> Warming of the Earth's atmosphere, land, and oceans due to excess greenhouse gases.

globalization
> The growth of the global economy and the interconnectedness of nations around the world.

greenhouse gases
> Gases in the Earth's atmosphere that trap heat; they include carbon dioxide, methane, and chlorofluorocarbons.

habitat
> The area where a plant or animal normally grows or lives.

industrialized
> To have or be dependent upon industry.

jet stream
> The long, narrow current of high-speed winds that affect weather patterns around the world.

recolonize
> To settle or populate again.

resilient
> Strong or able to recover from difficult conditions.

SOURCE NOTES

Chapter 1. A Warmer World

1. Caspar Ammann. Personal Interview. 15 Sept. 2006.
2. Ibid.
3. Barbara Kantrowitz and Karen Springen. "Will Polar Bears Be OK?" Newsweek. 16 April 2007.
4. Ibid.
5. Robert Roy Britt. "Insurance Company Warns of Global Warming's Costs." Live Science.com. 1 Nov. 2005. 27 July 2007 <http://www.livescience.com/environment/051101_insurance_warming.html>.
6. "Scientists Give Two Thumbs Up to Gore's Movie on Global Warming." USA Today. 27 June 2006. 5 July 2007 <http://www.usatoday.com/weather/news/2006-06-27-inconvenient-truth-reviews_x.htm>.
7. Ibid.

Chapter 2. The Path to Global Warming

1. Sean Markey. "Global Warming Has Devastating Effects on Coral Reefs, Study Shows." National Geographic. 16 May 2006. 27 July 2007 <www.news.nationalgeographic.com>.

Chapter 3. Studying Global Warming

1. David Frey. "Global Warming Good for Colorado Skiing?" Aspen Daily News. 17 June 2007.
2. Catherine Brahic. "Arctic Spring Arriving Weeks Earlier." Newscientist.com. 19 June 2007. <http://environment.newscientist.com/article/dn12091-arctic-spring-arriving-weeks-earlier.html>.
3. Chad Boutin. "Climate Model Forecasts Dramatic Changes in U.S." Purdue News Service. 17 Oct. 2005. 27 July 2007 <http://www.purdue.edu/UNS/html4ever/2005/051017.Diffenbaugh.model.html>.
4. Ibid.

Chapter 4. The Impact on Life on Earth

1. Randall Mikkelsen. "Arctic Tale Puts Faces to Global-Warming Threat." Reuters. 18 June 2007.
2. Monisha Bansal. "Animal group Blames Cat Influx on ... Global Warming?" CNSnews.com. 11 June 2007. 27 July 2007 <http://www.cnsnews.com/ViewCulture.asp?Page=/Culture/archive/20 0706/CUL20070611a.html>.
3. Ibid.
4. "Warming May Impact Asia-Pacific Region: Rising Temperatures Expected To Have Huge Impact In Asia-Pacific Region, Scientists Say." CBS News. 2 July 2007. 5 July 2007 <http://www.cbsnews.com/ stories/2007/07/02/ap/tech/main3010288.shtml>.
5. Lyon, Alistair. "Global warming to worsen refugee problem." 18 June 2007 <http://www.bangkokpost.com>.

Chapter 5. Changing Planet, Changing Climate

1. James Hansen, et al. "Global temperature change." Proceeding of the National Academy of Sciences of the United States of America. 25 Sept. 2006 <http://www.pnas.org/cgi/content/full/103/39/14288>.
2. John Young. "Black Water Rising." World Watch. 19.5 (2006): 26-31.
3. Al Gore. *An Inconvenient Truth*. Emmas, PA: Rodale. 2006. 149.
4. Emily Wax. "India's Sacred River Imperiled." The Washington Post. 17 June 2007.

Chapter 6. Ways to Limit Greenhouse Gases

1. "Stern Review: The Economics of Change." 16 July 2007 <http://news.bbc.co.uk/2/shared/bsp/hi/pdfs/30_10_06_exec_ sum.pdf>.
2. Robert Preston. "Report's Stark Warning on Climate." BBC News. 29 Oct. 2006. 17 July 2007 <http://news.bbc.co.uk/2/hi/business/ 6096594.stm>.
3. "100 billion invested in renewable energy in 2006." Mongobay.com. 20 June 2007 <http://news.mongabay.com/ 2007/0620-energy.html>.

SOURCE NOTES CONTINUED

4. "Carbon Capture and Storage to Combat Global Warming Examined." Science Daily. 12 June 2007. 12 July 2007. <http://www.Sciencedaily.com/releases/2007/06/070611153957.htm>.
5. Ibid.

Chapter 7. Policymakers Battle Global Warming

1. Fred Pearce. "Kyoto promises are nothing but hot air." New Scientist. 190. 2557 (2006): 10-11.
2. Sheryl Gay Stolberg. "Bush Proposes Goals on Greenhouse Gas Emissions." The New York Times. 1 June 2007.
3. Ibid.
4. Kurt Gottfried. "Re: Your quotes for global warming book." E-mail to the author. 6 Oct. 2006, 8 Oct. 2006, 10 Oct. 2006.
5. Juliet Eilperin. "Cities, States Aren't Waiting for U.S. Action on Climate." The Washington Post. 11 August 2006. 5 Oct. 2006 <www.washingtonpost.com/wp-dyn/content/article/2006/08/10/AR2006081001492_pf.html>.
6. "Western governors continue to focus on global warming." The Associated Press. 12 June 2007. 31 July 2007 <http://www.9news.com/news/politics_govt/article.aspx?storyid=71822>.

Chapter 8. What Organizations Are Doing

1. "Green Schools Initiative." Global Green USA. 25 Oct. 2006 <http://www.globalgreen.org/greenbuilding/GreenSchools.html>.
2. "Greenpeace Protests at UK Airports." The Associated Press. 19 June 2007.
3. Christopher Palmeri. "Conoco's Own Inconvenient Truth." Businessweekonline.com. 19 April 2007. 27 July 2007 <www.businessweek.com/bwdaily/dnflash/content/apr2007/db200704 19_165468.htm>.
4. Ibid.

Chapter 9. The Future of Global Warming

1. Dan Lashof. Natural Resources Defense Council. 16 Oct. 2006 <http://www.mixitproductions.com/prjsit/experts/lashq001.html#stopped>.

2. Stephen Schneider. "Re: PBS interview comments for middle school book on global warming." E-mail to author. 16 Oct. 2006.
3. "Global warming 'cannot be stopped'." Timesonline. 4 Sept. 2006. 16 Oct. 2006 <http://www.timesonline.co.uk/article/0,,2-2341516,00.html>.
4. John Crawley. "Senate seeks compromise on auto fuel standards." Reuters. 20 June 2007.
5. Jillian Micner. "Why 'Green' Investing Has Gained Focus. The Wall Street Journal. 21 June 2007.
6. David J. Lynch. "Corporate America Warms to Fight Against Global Warming." USA Today. 5 June 2006.
7. Ibid.

INDEX

ABOUT THE AUTHOR

Amy Farrar has been writing and editing for more than 20 years. She has a bachelor's degree in English from Rutgers University. Her articles have appeared in a variety of publications, including the *Los Angeles Times*. Farrar is a member and mentor of the Professional Editors Network in Minnesota. She also belongs to the Editorial Freelancers Association and the Society of Children's Book Writers and Illustrators. She lives in Minnesota.

PHOTO CREDITS

John McConnico/AP Images, cover, 3, 26; Missoulian, Michael Gallacher/AP Images, 6; Mary Altaffer/Ap Images, 15; Rodrigo Jana/AP Images, 16, 97 (bottom); Udo Weitz/AP Images, 25; Eric Miller/AP Images, 33; U.S. Fish and Wild Life Service, Steve Amstrup/AP Images, 34; David J. Phillip/AP Images, 36; Fernando Bustamante/AP Images, 43, 96; Karel Prinsloo/AP Images, 44; Jeff Barnard/AP Images, 48; Bikas Das/AP Images, 50; Luis M. Alvarez/AP Images, 53; Nick Ut/AP Images, 54, 97 (top); Casper Star-Tribune, Robert Hendricks/AP Images, 65; Ian Barrett/AP Images, 66, 95, 99 (top); Itsuo Inouye/AP Images, 69; Eriko Sugita/AP Images, 77, 98; Ryan Remiorz/AP Images, 78; LM Otero/AP Images, 82; Paul Sakuma/AP Images, 85; Thierry Charlier/AP Images, 86; Reed Saxon/AP Images, 91, 99 (bottom)